Michael Vick

By Jeff Savage

AMAZING ATHLETES

Lerner Publications Company • Minneapolis

Lerner Publications Company
A division of Lerner Publishing Group
241 First Avenue North
Minneapolis, MN 55401 U.S.A.

Website address: www.lernerbooks.com

Library of Congress Cataloging-in-Publication Data

Savage, Jeff, 1961–
      Michael Vick / by Jeff Savage.
          p.   cm. — (Amazing athletes)
      Includes index.
      ISBN-13: 978-0-8225-2430-4 (lib. bdg. : alk. paper)
      ISBN-10: 0-8225-2430-9 (lib. bdg. : alk. paper)
      1. Vick, Michael, 1980—Juvenile literature. 2. Football players—United States—Biography—
Juvenile I. Title. II. Series.
      GV939.V53S38 2006
      796.332'092—dc22   2005003113

Manufactured in the United States of America
1 2 3 4 5 6 – DP – 11 10 09 08 07 06

TABLE OF CONTENTS

Michael Vick drops back to throw a pass.

UNSTOPPABLE

The Atlanta Falcons had something to prove to their fans. They were facing the St. Louis Rams in the 2005 National Football League (NFL) **playoffs**. The Falcons had been a losing team for many years. They hardly ever made the playoffs. And the team made it to the **Super Bowl** only once. But in 2005, the Falcons had one hope. His name was Michael Vick.

Michael was just 24 years old. This was his third playoff game ever. But he was as cool as a **veteran** right from the start. On the third play of the game, Michael got loose from the Rams **defense** and ran for 47 yards. Michael is the fastest **quarterback** to ever play in the NFL. He is nearly unstoppable.

But Michael can throw too. Two plays later, he fired an 18-yard pass to **tight end** Alge Crumpler. Crumpler grabbed the ball for the game's first **touchdown**.

Michael does almost everything with his right hand. But he throws with his left hand.

Michael tries to break free from a Rams player.

In the second quarter, Michael led the Falcons down the field yet again. He dodged St. Louis players with his quick feet. He zipped a pass to **wide receiver** Brian Finneran. Then he fired a pass to receiver Michael Jenkins. Finally, he handed the ball to **running back** Warrick Dunn. Dunn raced into the **end zone** for the touchdown. Suddenly, the Falcons were ahead, 21–7.

The Rams were shocked. In the second half, Michael darted through the Rams defense. Falcons fans roared as Michael made more great plays. Atlanta won the game easily, 47–17. Michael had proved to millions of TV viewers that he was the next great football quarterback. "The whole world is watching," Michael said afterward. "This is a very exciting time for us."

Michael waves to the crowd after the Falcons' huge victory.

Michael's hometown is Newport News, Virginia. Michael's father worked in the city's shipyards.

LEARNING TO THROW

Michael Vick was born June 26, 1980, in Newport News, Virginia. He is the second of four children. His parents are Brenda Vick and

Michael Boddie. When Michael was born, his parents were not married and did not live together. Michael's father worked as a painter in the Newport News shipyards.

Brenda Vick raised her children in a three-bedroom apartment in downtown Newport News. To earn extra money for food and clothes, she drove a school bus. When Michael was nine, his parents got married. Michael kept his mother's name of Vick.

Michael grew up loving sports. He enjoyed playing football, baseball, and basketball with his friends.

Even as a youngster, Michael could throw the ball far. Warwick High School coach Tommy Reamon met Michael when he was a ninth grader. "I watched him zip that ball," Reamon remembers, "and I said 'Wow!'"

As a boy, Michael often played with his cousin Aaron Brooks. Aaron is the quarterback for the New Orleans Saints.

Coach Reamon saw that Michael had a chance to be a great player. He taught Michael how to get stronger by lifting weights.

He showed him how to build up his arm strength by throwing one hundred passes a day.

Coach Reamon also told Michael, "You must learn to read, write, and talk. As a quarterback in America, you must know how to communicate." Michael practiced at home by standing in front of a mirror and talking to himself.

The streets in the town where Michael grew up were not safe. Michael avoided trouble by going fishing. "I would go fishing even if the fish weren't biting," he said. "Just to get out of there."

When he wasn't playing football, Michael liked to go fishing. He also liked to play video games with his friends. But Michael loved football best. He was the starting quarterback at Warwick High for three years.

Michael's amazing speed and arm strength made him a great player. In three seasons, he passed for a whopping 4,846 yards and 43 touchdowns. He was also a great runner and scored 18 **rushing** touchdowns.

Michael's talents made him a star. Colleges from across the country invited him to play on their football teams. He chose Virginia Tech University in nearby Blacksburg, Virginia.

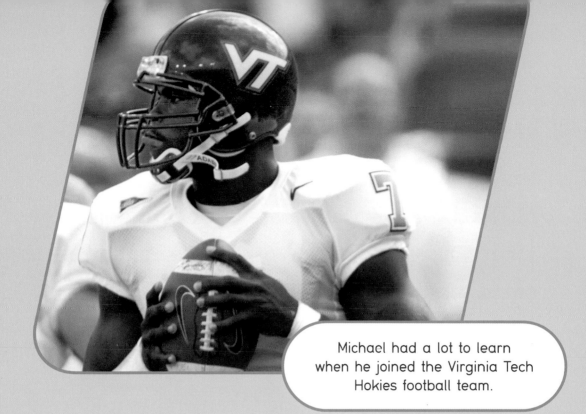

Michael had a lot to learn when he joined the Virginia Tech Hokies football team.

RUNNING OUT FRONT

Playing quarterback is a tough job. A quarterback has to spend many hours studying the team's **playbook**. He has to know what every player on his team is supposed to do on every play. He also has to guess what the other team's defense is going to do on each play.

The Virginia Tech coaches didn't allow Michael to play football his first year. Instead, they wanted him to learn the team's playbook. Michael watched tapes of games and went to meetings. He practiced with the team. But he stood on the sidelines during games.

The team's plays were so difficult that Michael grew frustrated. "I'm going to tell coach I want to play wide receiver," he told a teammate. "This is too much. I can't take it all in." The coaches told him to keep studying and be patient.

After his first year, Michael's hard work started to pay off. Coach Frank Beamer made Michael the **starter** at quarterback. In his first game of the 1999 season, he ran for three touchdowns. He led his team, the Virginia Tech Hokies, to a 47–0 victory.

Michael's amazing play made him big news. Everyone wanted to see this speedy quarterback and his powerful arm. He was one of the most exciting players in college football. As the season continued, Michael led the team to one win after another. The high point of the season came when the Hokies pounded the mighty Syracuse Orangemen 62–0.

The Hokies were unstoppable with Michael as the starting quarterback.

Michael's mom *(center)* is very proud of her son. Coach Beamer *(right)* helped Michael become a great quarterback.

Everyone praised Michael's play. His mother cried at home watching her son's games on TV. "Everything he does is so positive and just so good," she said. "I'm shocked myself, watching him run and throw that ball."

Coach Beamer admired Michael's football skills. But he also admired Michael as a person. "He's kind and polite," said the coach. "He is a good person."

With Michael in charge, the Hokies finished the regular season unbeaten. Their perfect record meant they would compete for the national championship. They faced superpower Florida State in the 2000 **Sugar Bowl**.

Florida State roared to a 28–7 lead. The Hokies were in trouble. Michael gathered his team around him. He said, "Somebody's gotta step up. I guess it's going to be me."

Michael runs for a big gain against the Florida State Seminoles in the 2000 Sugar Bowl.

Michael took over the game. He passed for 225 yards, including a 49–yard touchdown. He ran for 97 yards, including a 3-yard touchdown. He led Virginia Tech to a 29–28 lead. But the powerful Florida State team was just too strong. The Hokies lost the game, 46–29.

Michael sprints down the sideline for another huge gain. Michael played well, but the Hokies couldn't beat the powerful Florida State Seminoles.

NFL commissioner Paul Tagliabue congratulates Michael for being the first player taken in the 2001 NFL Draft.

FLYING HIGH

Michael enjoyed one more great year at Virginia Tech. Then he decided to join the NFL. The Atlanta Falcons chose Michael as the first pick in the 2001 NFL **Draft**.

Later, Michael signed a six-year **contract** with the Falcons. The Falcons would pay him $62 million. He was barely 20 years old.

Falcons coach Dan Reeves wanted Michael to take time to learn the pro game. So, once again, Michael spent most of his first year watching and learning. Chris Chandler started the season at quarterback. But Chandler was hurt midway through the season.

Michael *(center)* started his career with the Falcons by watching and learning.

Coach Dan Reeves gave Michael his first chance to play halfway through Michael's first season.

Coach Reeves decided to give Michael a shot. Michael's first game was against the Dallas Cowboys. He threw his first touchdown pass and also ran for 40 yards. Best of all, he led the Falcons to a 20–13 win.

After the season ended, the Falcons let Chandler leave the team. Michael would be the team's new starter at quarterback for 2002.

Michael had a terrific season his second year.

Michael took the NFL by storm in 2002. No one had ever seen such a mixture of speed and arm strength. When Michael **scrambled** with the ball, players struggled to catch and tackle him. And Michael's powerful passes shot right past them.

Michael's skills helped lead the Falcons to nine wins and a spot in the playoffs. His great play also won him a place in the **Pro Bowl**.

The Falcons faced the Green Bay Packers in the playoffs. Michael started the game hot. He helped the Falcons earn a quick 7–0 lead with a great pass to wide receiver Shawn Jefferson. Later in the first quarter, the Falcons struck for another score and a 14–0 lead. The Falcons won the game easily, 27–7.

Michael runs past Green Bay Packers players for a big gain. The Packers couldn't stop Michael throughout the game.

After the game ended, Packers quarterback Brett Favre walked up to Michael. Brett said to Michael, "I'm proud of you. You're going to be a superstar in this league."

The Falcons' playoff run ended the next week. The powerful Philadelphia Eagles defeated the Falcons. Yet Michael had shown that he could lead his team to victory. Could he lead the Falcons to the Super Bowl?

Packers star quarterback Brett Favre congratulates Michael after his great performance.

A broken leg ruined Michael's hopes for a great 2003 season.

MASTER STUDENT

Atlanta fans could hardly wait for the 2003 season. But things didn't go well from the start. Michael was hurt in a **preseason** game against the Baltimore Ravens. A hard tackle left him with a broken leg. Michael spent most of the season on the sidelines. The Falcons ended up with just 5 wins. They lost 11 games. Coach Reeves was fired.

The Falcons hired Jim Mora Jr. to be their coach for the 2004 season. Mora promised to make the Falcons winners again.

Michael zips past a New Orleans Saints player. One player called Michael "the fastest guy I've ever seen in a football stadium."

Michael is so fast and strong that it usually takes at least two people to tackle him.

With Michael healthy, it was easy for the coach to keep his promise. The Falcons won 11 games that year and then beat the Rams in the playoffs. But Michael and his teammates lost their next game to the Philadelphia Eagles.

Michael carries his son, Mitez, off the field after another win.

Still, the Falcons know they will have more chances to make it to the Super Bowl. Michael will carry the team far. He works hard to be the best. "All I have to do is prepare well, do the things my coaches tell me to do, and study, study, study," he says. "Then, there is no stopping me."

Selected Career Highlights

2004   Led all NFL quarterbacks with 902 yards rushing
Led the Falcons to an 11–5 record
Led the Falcons to a 47–17 playoff win over the St. Louis Rams
Selected to the Pro Bowl for second time

2003   Missed 11 games with a broken leg
Rushed for 141 yards in one game, the third-highest total for a
quarterback in NFL history

2002   Completed first 10 passes in first game against the Green Bay
Packers
Led the Falcons in scoring 17 points in the final 10 minutes to beat
the Pittsburgh Steelers
Ran 173 yards and set NFL record for most yards rushing by a
quarterback
Ran for 1,066 yards in his first two pro seasons, more than any
other quarterback
Led the Falcons to a 27–7 playoff victory against the Green Bay
Packers
Selected the to Pro Bowl for the first time

2001   First player selected overall in the NFL draft
In first pro start, threw a touchdown pass and rushed for 40 yards
to defeat the Dallas Cowboys

2000   Completed more than half his
passes
Passed for 1,234 yards
Rushed for 607 yards
Finished his Virginia Tech career
with a 20–1 regular season
record as a starter

1999   Led Virginia Tech to a perfect 11–0
regular season
Finished third in balloting for the
Heisman Trophy
Won the Archie Griffin Award as
college football Player of the Year

Glossary

contract: a written deal signed by a player and his or her team. The player agrees to play for the team for a certain number of years. The team agrees to pay the player a certain amount of money.

defense: the team of eleven players that doesn't have the football. The defense tries to stop the other team from scoring.

draft: a yearly event in which teams choose new players from a selected group

end zone: the area beyond the goal line at each end of the field. A team scores a touchdown when it reaches the other team's end zone.

playbook: a book that describes the plays a team will use in games

playoffs: a series of games held every year to decide a league champion

preseason: practice games played before the regular season begins

Pro Bowl: a game held every year after the season in which the best NFL players compete

quarterback: the football player whose job it is to pass the ball and call the plays. The quarterback is the leader of the offense.

running back: a player whose job it is to run with the ball

rushing: running with the football

scrambled: ran around with the ball before throwing it

starter: a person who is named to play from the beginning of the game

Sugar Bowl: a college football game played every year in the Super Dome in New Orleans, Louisiana.

Super Bowl: the NFL's championship game

tight end: a player who catches passes and blocks on rushing plays

touchdown: a six-point score. A team scores a touchdown when it gets into the other team's end zone with the ball.

veteran: a player who has played several seasons

wide receiver: a player who catches passes

Further Reading & Websites

Dougherty, Denis. *Michael Vick*. Edina, MN: Abdo Publishers, 2003.

Goodman, Michael, E. *The History of the Atlanta Falcons*. Mankato, MN: Creative Education, 2005.

The Official Site of the National Football League
http://nfl.com
The NFL's official website has news, scores, photos, video highlights, and information on all teams and players, including Michael Vick and the Atlanta Falcons.

The Official Website of Michael Vick
http://www.mikevick.com/
Michael's official website has the latest news, pictures, and a short biography of Michael.

Sports Illustrated for Kids
http://www.sikids.com
The *Sports Illustrated for Kids* website covers all sports, including NFL football.

Index

Photo Acknowledgments

Photographs are used with the permission of: © MARC SEROTA/Reuters/ Corbis, pp. 4, 6; © Streeter Lecka/Getty Images, p. 7; © Tim Wright/CORBIS, p. 8; © David Allio/Icon SMI/ZUMA press, p. 10; © Gary I. Rothstein/Icon SMI, p. 13; © Doug Pensinger/Allsport/Getty Images, p. 15; © AFP/Getty Images, p. 16; © Matthew Stockman/Getty Images, p.17; © Brian Bahr/Allsport/ Getty Images, p. 18; © Reuters/Corbis, p. 19; © Sportschrome East/West, Rob Tringali, pp. 20, 21, 22; © Jonathan Daniel/Getty Images, p. 23; © David Stluka/ Getty Images, p. 24; © Brenda J. Turner/ZUMA Press, p. 25; Dale Zanine/Icon SMI, p. 26; © Tami Chappell/Reuters/Corbis, p. 27; © Alan Mothner-US Presswire/ZUMA press, p. 28; © Darrell Walker/UTHM/Icon SMI, p. 29.

Front Cover: © Chris Livingston/Icon SMI